Zaner-Bloser

HANDWRITING

BASIC SKILLS and APPLICATION
Revised Edition

Book 6

WALTER B. BARBE, *Ph.D.*

Editor-in-Chief, *Highlights for Children*;
Adjunct Professor, The Ohio State University

VIRGINIA H. LUCAS, *Ph.D.*

Professor of Education
Wittenberg University, Springfield, Ohio

THOMAS M. WASYLYK

Master Penman and Handwriting Specialist;
Past President, International Association of Master Penmen,
Engrossers, and Teachers of Handwriting

CLINTON S. HACKNEY

Master Penman and Professional Handwriting Consultant,
Tampa, Florida

LOIS A. BRAUN

Supervisor, Elementary Curriculum,
Santa Monica-Malibu (California) Unified School District

The Old School House at St. Augustine, Florida. Built in the late 1700's, more than 50 years before Florida became a state, this is the only surviving colonial frame structure in the city. Hundreds of school children visit the building each year to see a recreated period schoolhouse with old desks, benches, and textbooks.

Do not write in this book.

Zaner-Bloser, Inc., Columbus, Ohio

The oldest city in the United States is St. Augustine, Florida. Ponce de Leon, in search of the Fountain of Youth, landed in 1513 and took possession of the territory for Spain. The flags of Spain, France, England, the Confederacy, and the United States have flown over this territory.

Write the paragraph on practice paper.

The oldest city in the United States is St. Augustine, Florida. Ponce de Leon, in search of the Fountain of Youth, landed in 1513 and took possession of the territory for Spain. The flags of Spain, France, England, the Confederacy, and the United States have flown over this territory.

✓ CHECK-UP

Evaluate your writing for these elements of legibility:

Letter formation

Spacing

Slant

Line quality

Alignment and proportion

Manuscript Check-Up

Write the letters in manuscript. Use practice paper.

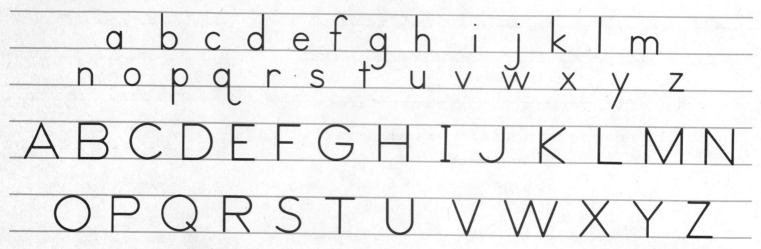

a b c d e f g h i j k l m
n o p q r s t u v w x y z

A B C D E F G H I J K L M N
O P Q R S T U V W X Y Z

1. Evaluate each of your letters for correct letter formation.

2. Which lower and upper-case letters are straight-line letters?

3. Which lower and upper-case letters are slant-line letters?

4. Which lower and upper-case letters are made with the backward circle?

5. Which lower and upper-case letters are made with the forward circle?

6. Check your letters for vertical alignment.

7. Circle any letters that need improvement.

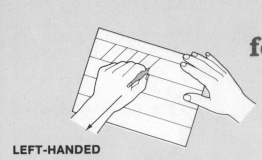

LEFT-HANDED

Paper Position
for Cursive Writing

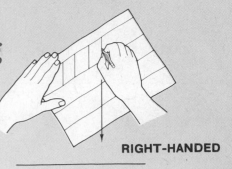

RIGHT-HANDED

Cursive Check-Up

Write the letters in cursive. Use practice paper.

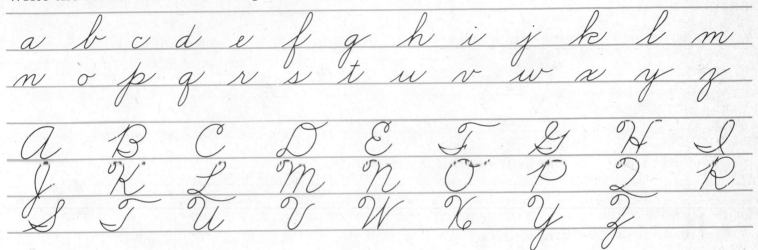

1. Evaluate each of your letters for correct letter formation.

2. Which fourteen lower-case letters begin with an undercurve?

3. Which eleven upper-case letters begin with a cane-stem?

4. Which two letters begin below the baseline?

5. How many maximum lower-case letters are there?

6. Check your letters for correct slant.

7. Circle any letters that need improvement.

Size and Proportion

MAXIMUM	INTERMEDIATE	MINIMUM	SLIGHTLY HIGHER
B f	*d p t*	*e a o*	*r s v w*

Maximum letters are almost the full-space height. They do not touch the headline. All the upper-case letters and the lower-case letters **b**, **f**, **h**, **k**, and **l** are maximum letters.

b f h k l

Write each letter three times on practice paper. Underline your best writing of each letter.

b C f G h K k W l Y
D E H I M N R S U P

Intermediate letters are two-thirds of the space height.

2/3 *d p t*

Write the letters and sentence on practice paper.
Underline your best writing of the letters **d**, **p**, and **t**.

d p t The average depth of the Atlantic Ocean is about 12,880 feet.

Minimum letters are one-third of the space height.

1/3 *a c e m n o w x i j g q y z*

Write each letter three times on practice paper.
Underline your best writing of each letter. Write the words.

a c e i y o n x
y z j g q m w
minimum courage serious
common sunrise nine

The minimum letters **r**, **s**, **v**, and **w** extend slightly above one-third of the space height.

1/3   *r s v w*

Write each letter three times on practice paper. Underline your best writing of each letter. Write the words.

r s v w   wrist   velvet   various

Descenders fill at least one-half of the space below the baseline.

f g j p q y z   *1/2*

Write the words on practice paper.
Use correct size and proportion.

design   brush   clay   palette
painter   colors   scaffold
Michelangelo   da Vinci

Write the sentences on practice paper.
Be sure to use the correct size and proportion.

The carpenters ate pound cake for dessert.

At a feast for sculptors, marble cake was served.

Carrot cake was served at the Farm Bureau's annual dinner.

✓ CHECK-UP

Check your writing for the following elements of legibility:

Maximum letters are the correct height.
Intermediate letters are the correct height.
Minimum letters are the correct height.
Descending letter loops are the correct length.

Spacing

This is an example of correct spacing. It makes your writing easier to read.

This is correct spacing. O It makes your writing easier to read.

Write the words on practice paper. Space each letter correctly.

spelling	*dictionary*	*minimum*
assignment	*English*	*paper*
vocabulary	*maximum*	*history*
lesson	*extended*	*world*

Write the sentences on practice paper.
Space them correctly.

In colonial schools, children read aloud together and answered in unison. Paper and pencils were not used. Each child had a slate to write on.

 CHECK-UP

Is your spacing between letters correct?

Is your spacing between words correct?

Is your spacing between sentences correct?

Noah Webster (1758-1843)

Noah Webster was the author of the first American Dictionary. He also wrote the first American spelling book, grammar book, and reader. As a teacher, journalist, lecturer, and lawyer, he found a need for a dictionary of American terms. It took Webster twenty years to compile the first American dictionary.

Webster simplified many British spellings in his American dictionary. The following are British spellings for words we commonly use today. On practice paper, write the American spellings for these words.

honour	*publick*	*favour*
musick	*centre*	*traffick*
litre	*academick*	*metre*

Dictionaries are constantly revised to include new words in our language. Write two sentences using three or more words that would not have been in Webster's first dictionary. Use practice paper.

For example:
She flew a single-engine plane equipped with radio, radar, and two parachutes.

 CHECK-UP

Is your spacing between letters correct?
Is your spacing between words correct?
Is your spacing between sentences correct?

Alignment and Line Quality

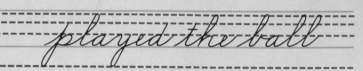

played the ball

Write the words on practice paper.

photograph	*pose*	*studio*
camera	*film*	*lights*
snapshot	*focus*	*prints*
shutter	*lens*	*flash*

LINE QUALITY

The writing should be smooth and even—not too dark, not too light.

smooth line quality

Write the sentences on practice paper. Evaluate for correct alignment and line quality.

Is a picture worth a thousand words?

Photographs record memories.

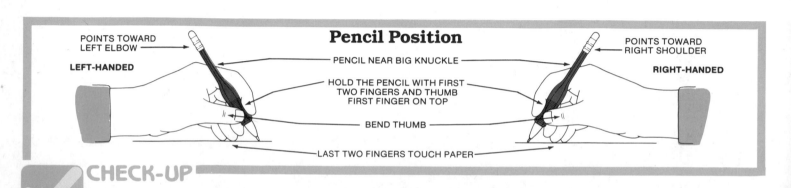

Pencil Position

POINTS TOWARD LEFT ELBOW

LEFT-HANDED

PENCIL NEAR BIG KNUCKLE

HOLD THE PENCIL WITH FIRST TWO FINGERS AND THUMB FIRST FINGER ON TOP

BEND THUMB

LAST TWO FINGERS TOUCH PAPER

POINTS TOWARD RIGHT SHOULDER

RIGHT-HANDED

CHECK-UP

Is your alignment correct?
Is your line quality correct?

DOROTHEA LANGE

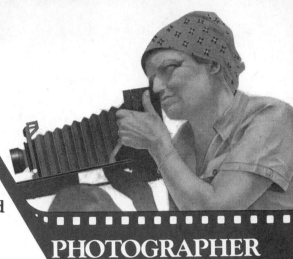

Dorothea Lange was interested in people. She took pictures of people who were hungry, ragged, homeless, and bewildered. Her pictures prodded others to offer help. People who saw her pictures cried, "Do something!" Dorothea was glad she caught these people on film and saved them for the world to see. "There is so much to see, to capture, which might never be there again."

PHOTOGRAPHER

Write the name of the famous photographer.

Dorothea Lange

If you were a photographer, write what you would like to take pictures of. Why? Use practice paper.

For example: *I would enjoy taking photographs of each new city or state I travel to. I would then arrange the pictures in an album and label them. This way I can keep a record of places I have been.*

 CHECK-UP

Is your alignment correct?
Is your line quality correct?

11

Slant

To check your slant, draw lines through the slant strokes. All slant lines should be parallel.

This is proper slant.

PARALLEL LINES

Proper slant is the result of correct:
1. paper position
2. direction downstrokes are pulled
3. shifting of paper.

Write the words. Evaluate the slant by drawing lines as you see in the example above. Use practice paper.

headline   *shift paper*   *slant*
parallel   *position*   *downstrokes*
baseline   *evaluate*   *spacing*

Write each of these sentences using proper slant. Use practice paper.

I must remember to position my paper correctly.

All my downstrokes must be pulled in the proper direction.

Paper Position

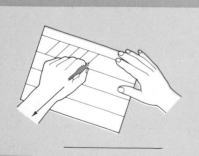

LEFT-HANDED

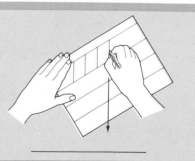

RIGHT-HANDED

Is the slant of your letters correct?

Poor Porcupine

Suppose he has an itchy place—
It must be quite a knack
For a porcupine to scratch it
With those needles on his back.

Florence Edick Sullivan

Write **true** or **false** for each statement
about porcupines. Use practice paper.

1. The porcupine feeds and wanders mostly at night.

2. The porcupine shoots its quills.

3. The porcupine eats the inner bark of pine trees.

4. The porcupine's entire body is covered with quills.

Write the poem "Poor Porcupine."

Use an encyclopedia to find more information on porcupines.

Is the slant of your writing correct?

Pauses in Lower-Case Letters

Rhythm (rith′ əm) n. The movement in letters determined by the pauses, loops, and directional changes.

A pause in writing occurs before a retrace or a sudden change of direction.

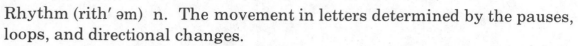

the tiny wingspread

A red dot (•) indicates a pause. A blue dot (•) indicates a lift.

This chart shows where each pause occurs in the lower-case letters.

a   b   c   d   e   f   g   h   i

j   k   l   m   n   o   p   q

r   s   t   u   v   w   x   y   z

Write each letter; then put a red dot (•) next to the pauses. Use practice paper.

a   b   c   d   e   f   g   h   i

j   k   l   m   n   o   p   q

r   s   t   u   v   w   x   y   z

Write the words on practice paper.
Write the number of pauses it takes to write each word.

fly   change   flutter

Across the sky, puffy white clouds dotted the blue heavens.
A circling hawk spread its shadow across the land below.

Migrating Monarchs

Write the sentences on practice paper.

In the fall, migrating monarchs start flying south. The butterflies in the midwestern United States and Canada go into southern Texas and into Mexico.

Write the meaning of the word **migrate**. Use practice paper.

migrate: to move from one country to another; to move seasonally from one area to another.

Write how you think monarch butterflies know when to migrate. Use practice paper.

Monarch butterflies know when to migrate because....

Place a dot (●) next to each pause in the lower-case letters you wrote.

Lower-Case Letters e, l, i, t, and j

Write the letters three times on practice paper.
Underline your best writing of each letter.

e   *l*   *i*   *t*   *j*

The letters **e, l, i, t,** and **j** begin with an undercurve.

The letters **e** and **l** are written without a pause. The letters **i**, **t**, and **j** are written with one pause and one lift. Count the rhythm as you trace each letter.

1 2 3	**1 2 3**	**1 and 2 3 4**	**1 and 2 3 4**	**1 and 2 3 4**

A red dot (•) indicates a pause. A blue dot (•) indicates a lift.

Count the rhythm as you write each letter.
Remember to say *and* at a pause.
Use practice paper.

e   *l*   *i*   *t*   *j*

Count the rhythm as you write each letter joining three times
on practice paper. Underline your best writing of each joining.

1 2 3 and 4 5 and 6 7	**1 2 3 4 5**	**1 and 2 3 4 and 5 6 and 7 8 9 10**	**1 and 2 3 and 4 5 6 7**	**1 and 2 3 and 4 5 and 6 and 7 8**
pause *ea*	no pauses *le*	pause *im* pause pause	pause → *ti* ← pause	pause → *jo* ← pause

Write the words on practice paper.

eager   *learn*   *time*   *tie*   *job*
pear   *file*   *climb*   *tire*   *joke*
ear   *let*   *trim*   *tile*   *jog*

16

The Gossamer Albatross

By Marshall MacCready

As a twelve-year-old, Marshall MacCready, son of the inventor, Paul MacCready, wrote this account of the first human-powered flight across the English Channel.

After my father won the $95,000 Kremer prize for a one-mile flight with the Gossamer Condor, people said it would be ten years before anyone would come close to winning the $210,000 Kremer prize for a human-powered flight across the English Channel. But my father took on[1] the challenge and built the lighter, more streamlined Gossamer Albatross.

On the night before the attempt[2], my father woke us in the middle of the night. I had gotten just[3] two hours of sleep. We went to the Warren, which is a long cement area right by the water. The parts of the Gossamer Albatross were stored[4] in a building there. The crew began[5] assembling the plane. My job[6] was to steady the front of the airplane.

About 5:00 AM on June 12, 1979, Bryan Allen, the pilot, started pedaling as hard as he could. The Albatross was only halfway along the runway when the front wheel broke. It took 45 minutes to fix. We tried again, and this time the plane

scraped the concrete a bit but made it off. Everybody cheered and clapped.

When the plane was out of view, my mother and I rushed over to the ferry. We didn't have time to buy tickets, but they quickly let us on. When the ferry landed in Bologne, France, we didn't know if the plane

had made it or not. We got a car to make the trip[7] to Cap Gris-Nez. We saw people carrying the plane and knew Bryan had made it.

The excitement was over, but I think I'll always remember[8] the day the Gossamer Albatross crossed the English Channel.

Write each numbered word in the story. Then write a synonym that begins with the letter given. Use practice paper.

1	took on	a	?
2	attempt	t	?
3	just	o	?
4	stored	k	?
5	began	s	?
6	job	a	?
7	trip	j	?
8	remember	r	?

17

ower-Case Letters f, g, a, d, h, and c

Write the letters three times on practice paper.
Underline your best writing of each letter.

f   g   a   d   h   c

The letters **f, g, a, d, h,** and **c** are written with one pause.

These letters are written with one pause.

1 2 3 and 4	1 2 and 3 4	1 2 and 3 4	1 2 and 3 4	1 2 and 3 4 5	1 and 2 3

A red dot (•) indicates a pause. A blue dot (•) indicates a lift.

Count the rhythm as you write each letter. Remember to say *and*
at a pause. Write the words. Use practice paper.

f   g   a   d   h   c

flag   gathered   addition   change

Count the rhythm as you write each letter joining three times
on practice paper. Underline your best writing of each joining.

1 2 3 and 4 and 5 6 7	1 2 and 3 4 5 6 7	1 2 and 3 4 5 and 6 7 8	1 2 and 3 4 and 5 6 and 7 8	1 2 and 3 4 5 and 6 7 and 8 and 9	1 and 2 3 and 4 5 and 6 7
pause	pause	pause	pause pause pause	pause	pause
fi	*ge*	*an*	*da*	*ho*	*cu*
pause		pause		pause pause	

Write the words on practice paper.

first   final   fig   fire

gear   ant   get   age

and   page   land   fan

date   dairy   damp   pedal

hope   home   host   photo

cure   cute   rescue   curt

18

Careers

No house should ever be on a hill or on anything. It should be of the hill, belonging to it, so hill and house could live together each the happier for....

● Frank Lloyd Wright, architect

I really believe there are things nobody would see if I didn't photograph them. But.... ● Diane Arbus, photographer

I ran because someone had to do it first. In this country everyone is supposed to be able to run for President, but that's never been really true. Someday....

●Shirley Chisolm, Congresswoman, candidate for President,1972

Improvisation is a form of self-expression, and it's very gratifying to improvise in front of people. I feel I'm including them in what I'm doing, taking them someplace they might like to go and haven't been before. Of course.... ● Jim Hall, jazz guitarist

...most people prefer to carry out the kinds of experiments that allow the scientist to feel that he is in full control of the situation rather than....

● Margaret Mead, anthropologist

All good books are alike in that they are truer than if they had really happened and after you are finished reading one you will feel that all that happened to you and afterwards it all belongs to you.... If you can get so that you can give that to people, then....

● Ernest Hemingway, writer

Read the quotes above. Choose one and write an ending for it.

For example:

...so hill and house could live together each the happier for its close bonding to the other — inseparable and blended.

Circle the letters **f, h, a, d, g,** and **c** in your writing.
Are they formed correctly?

Match the rhythm count with the letter joining. Write a word using each of the letter joinings. Use practice paper. A red *and* indicates a pause. A blue numeral indicates a lift.

COUNT	LETTER JOINING	WORD
1. 1 2 3 and 4 and 5 6 7	*ea*	*each*
2. 1 and 2 3 and 4 5 and 6 7	*le*	*left*
3. 1 2 and 3 4 and 5 6 and 7 8	*il*	*oil*
4. 1 2 3 and 4 5 and 6 7	*fi*	*fine*
5. 1 and 2 3 4 5 6	*ha*	*half*
6. 1 2 and 3 4 5 6	*te*	*tent*
7. 1 2 and 3 4 5 and 6 7 and 8 9	*dg*	*dodge*
8. 1 and 2 3 4 5 6	*ja*	*jar*
9. 1 2 3 4 5	*ca*	*case*
10. 1 and 2 3 and 4 5 and 6 7 8	*ge*	*gauge*

Write a sentence using some of the words you wrote. Use practice paper.

For example: *The oil gauge showed half a quart left.*

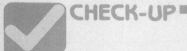

Evaluate your writing for these elements of legibility:
Letter formation
Slant
Spacing
Alignment and proportion
Line quality

20

WINNERS

Katharine Hepburn   **Boris Becker**   **Michael Jackson**   **Tiffany Chin**   **Gwendolyn Brooks**

Write the names of these famous people with their achievements.
Write in manuscript on practice paper.

Eight Grammy Awards--
Pulitzer Prize for Poetry--
Wimbledon Tennis Champion
Academy Award--
Figure Skating Champion--

Nadia Comaneci
Olympic Gold Medalist

Write the following quotation of Nadia Comaneci in manuscript.
Use practice paper.

"Be prepared to work hard every day. Working hard is the difference between being good and being the best."

There are many people who never receive awards or special recognition but have achieved greatness in their own way. Write in manuscript what you think makes a person a success.

I think a person becomes a success by...

Is your letter formation correct?
Is your vertical quality correct?

Writing Numerals

Write the numerals three times on practice paper. Underline your best writing of each.

1   2   3   4   5   6   7   8   9   10

Be sure all your numerals have correct slant.

Numerals are approximately one-half the space height. Count the rhythm as you trace each numeral. A red dot (•) indicates a pause. A blue dot (•) indicates a lift.

1	*2*	*3*	*4*	*5*	*6*	*7*	*8*	*9*	*10*
1	1 and 2 and 3	1 and 2 and 3	and 2 3	1 and 2 3	1 2 3	1 and 2 and 3	1 2 3	1 2 and 3	1 2 3

Count the rhythm as you write each numeral.
Remember to say *and* at a pause. Use practice paper.

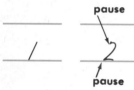

1   2   3   4   5   6   7   8   9   10

Write the decimals and add. Remember to line up
the decimal points. Use practice paper.

1. 234.5612 + 128.9064 + 398.7755
 + 123.4567 + 983.6704 =

2. 1462.8 + 7815.2 + 5670.8 + 1955.1
 + 6382.4 =

3. 1689.12 + 6345.78 + 9012.43 + 1875.68
 + 7921.64 =

4. 5462.158 + 4301.221 + 6549.301
 + 9616.001 + 8754.321 =

22

Filling Out Forms

What problems may result from the way this form
has been completed?

Department of the Treasury—Internal Revenue Service

Employee's Withholding Allowance Certificate

W-4
(October 1979)

Your social security number ▶ 288 74 7856

your full name ▶ *Paula Jo Smith*

ess (including ZIP code) ▶ *1688 Boulevard East Guttenberg, N.J. 69678*

Date ▶ *8/23/1990* , 19

ployee's signature ▶ *Paula Jo Smith*

Write the information asked for in the application below. Use practice paper.

INSTRUCTIONS TO APPLICANT ▶	Complete this form. Use your best writing.		
NAA **1** NAME TO BE SHOWN ON CARD	First	Middle	Last
STT **2** MAILING ADDRESS	(Street/Apt. No., P.O. Box, Rural Route No.)		
CTY STE ZIP CITY		STATE	ZIP CODE

DOB **3** DATE OF BIRTH ▶	MONTH	DAY	YEAR	**AGE** **4**	PRESENT AGE	**PLB** **5**	PLACE OF BIRTH ▶	CITY	STATE OR FOREIGN COUNTRY

DON **6** TODAY'S DATE ▶	MONTH	DAY	YEAR	**7**	Telephone number where we can reach you during the day ▶	HOME	OTHER

ASD **8** YOUR SIGNATURE	

Complete the Social Security card with your name and any nine digits
for a Social Security Number.

SOCIAL SECURITY

267-28-3496

THIS NUMBER HAS BEEN ESTABLISHED FOR

Virginia H. Lucas

Virginia H. Lucas
SIGNATURE

SOCIAL SECURITY

THIS NUMBER HAS BEEN ESTABLISHED FOR

Write the information
on practice paper.

SIGNATURE

Lower-Case Letters n, y, z, and x

Write the letters three times on practice paper.
Underline your best writing of each letter.

n   *y*   *z*   *x*

The letters **n**, **y**, **z**, and **x** begin with an overcurve.

The letters **n**, **y**, and **z** are written with one pause. The letter **x** is written with one lift.

1 2 and 3 4 5	1 2 3 and 4 5	1 2 and 3 4	1 2 3 4

A red dot (•) indicates a pause. A blue dot (•) indicates a lift.

Count the rhythm as you write each letter. Remember to say *and*
at a pause. Use practice paper.

n   *y*   *z*   *x*

Count the rhythm as you write each letter joining three times
on practice paper. Underline your best writing of each joining.

1 2 and 3 4 5 and 6 7 and 8 9	1 2 3 and 4 5 and 6 7 and 8 and 9	1 2 and 3 4 and 5 6 and 7 and 8	1 2 3 and 4 5 6 7
pause / pause	pause / pause	pause / pause / pause	pause
nu	*yo*	*zo*	*xi*

Write the words on practice paper.

nurse   *your*   *zoo*   *axis*

nut   *yodel*   *zone*   *taxi*

Steps to Writing

a mystery to solve
an exciting adventure

growing up
the funniest thing that ever happened

my favorite book
a zookeeper's nightmare

1 Select a topic.

Choose a topic from above or use one of your own.

2 List ideas.

List characters, objects,

situations, and descriptive

phrases to develop your topic.

3 Arrange Ideas in order.

Organize all your ideas by

listing them in order. Think

of an interesting title.

4 Prepare a rough draft on practice paper.

Take the ideas you have arranged in order

and write them on paper in sentence form.

5 Proofread.

Carefully read what you have written. Check for correct punctuation,

capitalization, and correct grammar. Combine short sentences into

longer ones. Substitute synonyms for words you may use often.

6 Write a final copy.

Rewrite your paragraph or story. Give it a title.

Lower-Case Letters u, p, k, b, and s

Write the letters three times on practice paper.
Underline your best writing of each letter.

u   *p*   *k*   *b*   *s*

The letters **u, p, k, b,** and **s** are written with two pauses.

These letters are written with two pauses.

1 and 2 3 and 4 5	1 and 2 3 4 and 5	1 2 and 3 4 and 5 6	1 2 3 and 4 and 5	1 and 2 and 3

A red dot (•) indicates a pause. A blue dot (•) indicates a lift.

Count the rhythm as you write each letter.
Remember to say *and* at a pause. Use practice paper.

u   *p*   *k*   *b*   *s*

Count the rhythm as you write each letter joining three times
on practice paper. Underline your best writing of each joining.

1 and 2 3 and 4 5 and 6 7 8	1 and 2 3 4 and 5 and 6 7 8	1 2 and 3 4 and 5 6 7 8	1 2 3 and 4 and 5 6 7 and 8 9	1 and 2 and 3 and 4 5 and 6 7
pause	pause		pause	pause
ui	*pi*	*ke*	*by*	*sa*
	pause	pause	pause	pause

Write the words on practice paper.

ruins	*piece*	*key*	*bye*	*safe*
fluid	*pipe*	*keep*	*baby*	*sat*
bake	*supper*	*peak*	*soak*	*skunk*

26

Descriptive Writing

Choose a character and a setting from the lists.
Write four words that might describe each. Use practice paper.

Character
biologist
sailor
king
umpire
pilot

Follow this model:

Setting
imaginary world
outer space
baseball field
mucky swamp
sinking ship

Character

sailor

Setting

sinking ship

Descriptive Words

fearless
strong
tall
suntanned

Descriptive Words

battered
weather-beaten
rocking
overturned

Write a short paragraph on practice paper using
the character and setting you have chosen.

The tall sailor knew the battered ship was sinking as the wind and waves tossed the rocking boat. The fearless crew had tried to save the overturned ship.

Lower-Case Letters q, o, m, v, r, and w

Write the letters three times on practice paper.
Underline your best writing of each letter.

q   *o*   *m*

v   *r*   *w*

The letters **q**, **o**, **m**, and **v** are written with two pauses. The letter **r** is written with three pauses. The letter **w** is written with four pauses. Count the rhythm as you trace each letter.

1 2 and 3 4 and 5	1 2 and 3 and 4	1 2 and 3 4 and 5 6 7	1 2 3 and 4 and 5	1 and 2 and 3 and 4 5	1 and 2 3 and 4 5 and 6 and 7

A red dot (•) indicates a pause.   A blue dot (•) indicates a lift.

Count the rhythm as you write each letter. Remember to say *and* at a pause. Use practice paper.

q   *o*   *m*

v   *r*   *w*

Count the rhythm as you write each letter joining three times
on practice paper. Underline your best writing of each joining.

1 2 and 3 4 and 5 and 6 7 and 8 9	1 2 and 3 and 4 and 5 6 and 7 8	1 2 and 3 4 and 5 6 7 and 8 9 and 10 11	1 2 3 and 4 and 5 6 7	1 and 2 and 3 and 4 5 6 7 and 8 9	1 and 2 3 and 4 5 and 6 and 7 and 8 and 9 and 10 11
pause / *qu* / pause	pause / *oa* / pause	pause / *ma* / pause	pause / *ve* / pause	pause / *ry* / pause	pause / pause / *wy* / pause

Write the words on practice paper.

quart	*quail*	*quiet*	*quit*
oasis	*toast*	*loan*	*boat*
mask	*man*	*made*	*may*
vex	*vest*	*pave*	*save*
rye	*hurry*	*very*	*merry*
wrist	*wrote*	*wring*	*wren*

Write the letters and letter combinations on practice paper.

Add one or more letters to make a word.

Score: number of letters in word

q qu qui	quintuplets	11
o ou out		
m mi mis	Begin by folding	
v va val	your practice	
r ro roo	paper into 3	
w wh whe	columns. Write	
q qu qua	in each column as	
o ov ove	shown in the	
m mo mon	example. Total	
v vi vic	your score at the	
r re res	end.	
w we wea		
	Total	

Circle the lower-case letters **q, o, m, v, r,** and **w** in your writing.
Do they match the models on page 28?

Pauses in Upper-Case Letters

Pauses determine good rhythm and fluency. To write with good rhythm and fluency, sit comfortably and relaxed. Be sure that your paper is in the correct position and that you shift the paper as your writing progresses across the page.

A pause in an upper-case letter is determined by a retrace or a sudden change of direction.

Rhythm   *B*   *T*

A red dot (•) indicates a pause. A blue dot (•) indicates a lift.

This chart shows where each pause and lift occurs in the upper-case letters.

A B C D E F G H I
J K L M N O P Q R
S T U V W X Y Z

Write each letter and show the pauses and lifts. Use practice paper.

A B C D E F G H I
J K L M N O P Q R
S T U V W X Y Z

Write each letter that does not have a pause.

C D E J K L O Q U X Z

Write each letter that has more than one pause.

B F G M P R W

Write each letter that contains a lift.

F H K T X

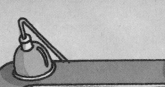

Names You Know

Find the names in the puzzle that begin with the letters given below. Write the names in cursive.

```
L X M N V T A L L L Y O Y Y A P D E J O P S K Y F T Y I
U A L O O N E Z F Z D Q A T F R E D T O C U E E H S D
N I O N Y K M R M J A D U S T V F U L F S V N I O Z A
A T A L P X Y B E O K E L I O A R R M Z A L E T R E H
O E L L E N O K R S L I A K N R A N C D Y C R V I O F
Y A J S I B G W E L A L D Y V C V Y K C L T D I Q N L
W R N N T R I P V E I L Y N L B Y K E M L T Q F V A G
G K A R E N D W I E T D L T E O W C L H A R R Y H N I
P A T T Y T D A L Y Z L V I C W Y I A F S H J T S C V
R G I W M H N D O X A V I E R E G V Z U N A D Y L Y I
```

The first two letters in each name are given as clues. Write on practice paper.

A	Al	J	Ja	S	Sa
B	Bo	K	Ka	T	Te
C	Ca	L	Lo	U	Un
D	Da	M	Mo	V	Vi
E	El	N	Na	W	Wa
F	Fr	O	Ol	X	Xa
G	Gw	P	Pa	Y	Yo
H	Ha	Q	Qu	Z	Za
I	Id	R	Ro		

Upper-Case Letters C, D, E, and O

Write the letters three times on practice paper.
Underline your best writing of each letter.

C   *D*   *E*   *O*

These letters are written without a pause.

1 2 3 *C*   **1 2 3 4** *D*   **1 2 3 4** *E*   **1 2 3** *O*

Count the rhythm as you write each letter on practice paper.

C **1 2 3**   *D* **1 2 3 4**   *E* **1 2 3 4**   *O* **1 2 3**

Count the rhythm as you write each letter joining three times
on practice paper. Underline your best writing of each joining.

1 2 3 and 4 5 and 6 7   **1 2 3 4 5 6 and 7 8**   **1 2 3 4 5 6**   **1 2 3 4 and 5 and 6**

pause   pause   no pauses   pause

Ca   *Da*   *El*   *Os*

pause

Write the words on practice paper.

Carmen   *Daniel*   *Eloise*   *Oscar*
Chris   *David*   *Elena*   *Olivia*
Connie   *Denise*   *Ed*   *Ollie*

Write the sentence on practice paper. Underline the word that has the most pauses.

Eleven elephants will arrive COD in tomorrow morning's shipment.

32

Diamante

A diamante is a diamond-shaped poem.
Lines one and seven contain opposite
nouns. **Lines two and six** each contain two
adjectives describing the noun nearest the
line. **Lines three and five** provide three
participles (*ing* words) describing the noun
nearest the line. **Line four** gives two nouns
for each.
Write the diamante.

Ocean
salty, wet
rolling, crashing, pulling
water, waves, sun, sand
sparkling, spreading, baking
hot, dry
Desert

Earth

Create your own diamante using **Earth** for line one and **Clouds** for line seven.

Write your diamante on practice paper.

Clouds

Are your upper-case letters **C, D, E,** and **O** formed correctly?

Upper-Case Letters J, L, Q, V, and Z

Write the letters three times on practice paper.
Underline your best writing of each letter.

J   *L*   *Q*   *V*   *Z*

The letters **J, L, Q, V,** and **Z** are written without a pause.

These letters are written without a pause.

123   123   123   1234   12345

Count the rhythm as you write each letter on practice paper.

J   *L*   *Q*   *V*   *Z*

Count the rhythm as you write each letter joining three times
on practice paper. Underline your best writing of each joining.

1 2 3 and 4 5 and 6 7 | 1 2 3 4 and 5 6 7 | 1 2 3 4 and 5 6 and 7 8 | 1 2 3 4 5 6 7 | 1 2 3 4 5 and 6 7 and 8 and 9

pause   pause   pause   no pauses   pause

Ja   *Li*   *Qu*   *Ve*   *Zo*

Write the words on practice paper.

January   *Jamaica*   *James*
Louisiana   *Lincoln*   *Libya*
Quebec   *Queens*   *Quincy*
Venus   *Venezuela*   *Vesta*
Zola   *Zora*   *Zoltan*

34

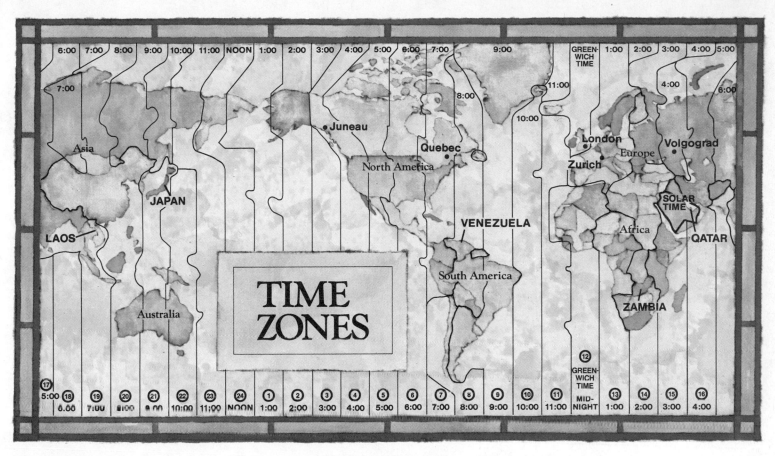

On practice paper, write the times listed below. Using the map above, write the name of the country or city next to the correct time if it is 12:00 midnight Greenwich time.

Time	Country
2:00 A.M.	?
7:00 A.M.	?
9:00 A.M.	?
8:00 P.M.	?

Time	City
1:00 A.M.	?
4:00 A.M.	?
4:00 P.M.	?
7:00 P.M.	?

Which country is in the solar time zone?

Which city is in the Greenwich time zone?

CHECK-UP   Circle the upper-case letters in your writing.
Do they match the models on page 34?

The ease with which one's writing can be read is the best test of its legibility. One poorly written letter may cause difficulty.

Write the above sentences and evaluate your writing for each element of legibility.

Use practice paper.

Remember, the elements of legibility are **letter formation, slant, spacing, alignment and proportion,** and **line quality**.

Circle the letters **i, r, s, t, w, y, m, p,** and **u** in the sentences you wrote. Underline the circled letters that are formed correctly.

Write the rhythm count of each letter. Use practice paper.

g   *C*
j   *D*
k   *E*
v   *F*
x   *L*
y   *Z*

✓ CHECK-UP

Evaluate your writing for these elements of legibility:
Letter formation
Slant
Spacing
Alignment and proportion
Line quality

Helen Keller by Nita Cain

Helen Keller lived her life without seeing or hearing. She had a very special teacher named Anne Sullivan.

During her first day with Helen, Anne spelled out the word *doll* into Helen's hand. Helen soon learned to spell words into Anne's hand, but to Helen this game had no meaning. Then one scorching day, Helen placed her hands under the cooling water at the pump, and Anne spelled *water* into her hand. Helen remembers: "Suddenly I felt a misty consciousness of something forgotten—a thrill of returning thought; and somehow the mystery of language was revealed to me."

This is the Braille code invented by Louis Braille. It is a code of small raised dots.

a	b	c	d	e	f	g	h	i
j	k	l	m	n	o	p	q	r
s	t	u	v	w	x	y	z	

Use the Braille code to figure out the words below. Write them on practice paper.

Two activities Helen enjoyed were:

Upper-Case Letters A, N, I, and S

Write the letters three times on practice paper.
Underline your best writing of each letter.

$\mathcal{A}$ $\mathcal{N}$ $\mathcal{I}$ $\mathcal{S}$

These letters are written with one pause.

1 2 and 3 4   **1 2 3 and 4 5 6**   **1 2 3 and 4**   **1 2 3 and 4**

A red dot (•) indicates a pause. A blue dot (•) indicates a lift.

Count the rhythm as you write each letter on practice paper.
Remember to say *and* at a pause.

$\mathcal{A}$ $\mathcal{N}$ $\mathcal{I}$ $\mathcal{S}$

Count the rhythm as you write each letter joining three times
on practice paper. Underline your best writing of each joining.

1 2 and 3 4 5 and 6 7 and 8 9   **1 2 3 and 4 5 6 7 8**   **1 2 3 and 4 5 6 and 7 and 8**   **1 2 3 and 4 5 6 and 7 8**

pause   *Ak*   *Ne*   *Io*   *Sa*

Write the words on practice paper.

Akron   Nevada   Iowa   Salina

Akim   Neil   Iona   Sally

Alberto   Neva   Italy   Susan

Write the sentence on practice paper. Underline the word that has the most pauses.

Sir Isaac Newton is best known for his theory of gravitation.

Write this sentence in cursive.

Abraham Lincoln ran for the U. S. Senate from Illinois.

Writing Dialogue

"You can have one if you can get it home."

"It's too little, Abe. It'll never eat."

"You'll have to take it back. You can't let the little thing starve."

On practice paper, write the missing dialogue.

Neighbor: You can have one if you can get it home.

What did Abe reply?

Abe's Mother: It's too little, Abe. It'll never eat.

What did Abe reply?

Abe's Mother: You'll have to take it back. You can't let

the little thing starve.

What did Abe reply?

Every day Abe made the trip back to the neighbor's farm for the young pig's dinner.

Upper-Case Letters U, Y, K, and X

Write the letters three times on practice paper. Underline your best writing of each letter.

$\mathcal{U}$ $\mathcal{Y}$ $\mathcal{K}$ $\mathcal{X}$

The letters **U**, **Y**, **K**, and **X** begin with a cane-stem stroke.

The letters **U** and **Y** are written with one pause. The letters **K** and **X** are written with one lift.

1 2 3 4 and 5 6   1 2 3 4 and 5 6   1 2 3 4 5 6   1 2 3 4 5 6

A red dot (•) indicates a pause.   A blue dot (•) indicates a lift.

Count the rhythm as you write each letter on practice paper.
Remember to say *and* at a pause.

$\mathcal{U}$ $\mathcal{Y}$ $\mathcal{K}$ $\mathcal{X}$

Count the rhythm as you write each letter joining three times on practice paper. Underline your best writing of each.

1 2 3 4 and 5 6 and 7 8 9	1 2 3 4 and 5 6 and 7 8 and 9 and 10	1 2 3 4 5 6 and 7 8 and 9 10	1 2 3 4 5 6 7 8 9
pause	pause	pause	no pauses
$\mathcal{Ut}$	$\mathcal{Yo}$ pause	$\mathcal{Ka}$	$\mathcal{Xe}$

Write the words on practice paper.

$\mathcal{Utah}$ $\mathcal{Yolanda}$ $\mathcal{Kansas}$ $\mathcal{Xenia}$
$\mathcal{Utrillo}$ $\mathcal{York}$ $\mathcal{Kate}$ $\mathcal{Xerxes}$

Write the sentence on practice paper. Underline the word that has the most pauses.

Please call Ursula, Yvette, Kurt, and Xavier
to tell them about the softball game.

Dreams
by Langston Hughes

Hold fast to dreams
For if dreams die
Life is a broken-winged bird
That cannot fly.

What are your dreams and goals for the future?
Read the poem "Dreams" by Langston Hughes.
To what does he compare a life without dreams?
Write these sentences in cursive on practice paper.

"Dreams" is from a collection of poems called The Dream Keeper. When the author, Langston Hughes, received his degree from Lincoln University, his first two books had already been published. Young Hughes had also received many awards.

Write a paragraph about your dream or goal on practice paper.

 CHECK-UP

Are your upper-case letters **D, K, L, U,** and **Y** formed correctly?

Upper-Case Letters H, M, P, R, G, and T

Write the letters three times on practice paper. Underline your best writing of each letter.

The letters **G**, **M**, **P**, and **R** are written with two pauses. The letters **H** and **T** are written with one pause and one lift. Count the rhythm as you trace each letter.

| 1 2 and
3 4 and 5 | 1 2 3 and 4 5
and 6 7 8 | 1 and 2 and 3 4 | 1 and 2 and
3 4 5 6 | 1 2 3 4 and | 1 2 and 3 4 5 |

A red dot (•) indicates a pause. A blue dot (•) indicates a lift.

Count the rhythm as you write each letter on practice paper. Remember to say *and* at a pause.

Count the rhythm as you write each letter joining three times
on practice paper. Underline your best writing of each joining.

| 1 2 and 3 4 and 5 6
and 7 8 and 9 10 | 1 2 3 and 4 5 and
6 7 8 9 10 | 1 and 2 and
3 4 5 6 and 7 8 | 1 and 2 and 3 4 5 6
and 7 8 and 9 and 10 | 1 2 3 4 and 5 6 and
7 8 and 9 10 | 1 2 and 3 4 5 6
and 7 8 9 |

Write the words on practice paper.

Guam   Guatemala   Rosa
Mexico   Memphis   Melville
Paris   Panama   Pandora
Rome   Roosevelt   Gulfport
Hawaii   Hamburg   Handel
Tivoli   Tibet   Titian

42

PLACES TO TRAVEL

If you sent these postcards, how would you describe each sight? Write the names of the places and your descriptions.

Pyramids

Write on practice paper.

Grand Canyon

Taj Mahal

Hawaii

Use the encyclopedia to find information about these places.

43

Upper-Case Letters B, F, and W

Write the letters three times on practice paper.
Underline your best writing of each letter.

$\mathcal{B}$ $\mathcal{F}$ $\mathcal{W}$

The letters **B** and **W** are written with three pauses. The letter **F** is written with two pauses and one lift.

1 and 2 and 3 4 5 and 6   **1 2 and 3 and 4 5 6**   **1 2 3 and 4 and 5 and 6**

A red dot (•) indicates a pause. A blue dot (○) indicates a lift.

Count the rhythm as you write each letter on practice paper.
Remember to say *and* at a pause.

$\mathcal{B}$ $\mathcal{F}$ $\mathcal{W}$

Count the rhythm as you write each letter joining three times
on practice paper. Underline your best writing of each joining.

1 and 2 and 3 4 5 and 6 7 8 and 9 10	1 and 2 and 3 4 5 and 6 7 8 9	1 2 and 3 and 4 5 6 7 and 8 9 10	1 2 and 3 and 4 5 6 7 8 and 9 and 10	1 2 3 and 4 and 5 and 6 7 8 9	1 2 3 and 4 and 5 and 6 7 and 8 9 and 10 11
pause $\mathcal{Ba}$	pause $\mathcal{Be}$	pause $\mathcal{Fi}$	pause $\mathcal{Fo}$	pause $\mathcal{We}$	pause $\mathcal{Wi}$

Write the words on practice paper.

$\mathcal{Bach}$ $\mathcal{Bell}$ $\mathcal{Fiji}$ $\mathcal{Fox}$ $\mathcal{West}$
$\mathcal{Baltic}$ $\mathcal{Ben}$ $\mathcal{Fidel}$ $\mathcal{Ford}$ $\mathcal{Welsh}$

Write the sentences on practice paper. Underline the word that has the most pauses.

Barbara:	*Find Beethoven's teacher.*
Frank:	*Why? Is he hidin'?*
Barbara:	*Yes, he is Franz Joseph Haydn.*

44

Flatboats

A flatboat is a rectangular wooden raft-like boat, complete with a cabin and high sides. Flatboats went only one way—downstream with the current.

Flatboats were easy and inexpensive to build, and they could be taken apart at the end of the journey and used for building homes.

Frank, Beth, and their children, Walter and Barbara, are taking a trip down the Ohio River to find a new home. Imagine you are on the flatboat with them. Write about a day on the flatboat. Use practice paper.

You may wish to include some of the following ideas:

strong river current
thick, unexplored forests
trapper's cabin
campfires at night
friendly pioneer families
plentiful wildlife

Evaluate your writing for these elements of legibility:

Letter formation
Slant
Spacing

Alignment and proportion
Line quality

Write each upper-case letter in cursive. Use practice paper.

A B C D E F G H I
J K L M N O P Q
R S T U V W X Y Z

Put a red dot (•) at each pause and a blue dot (•) at each lift in the letters above.

On practice paper, write the correct numeral for each rhythm count.

Use each numeral only once.

1 and 2 and 3	1 2 3	1 2 3	1 and 2 and 3	1 2 3
?	?	?	?	?

1 and 2 3	1 2 and 3	1	1 and 2 and 3	1 and 2 3
?	?	?	?	?

Write the sentence on practice paper.

To write with good rhythm and fluency, sit comfortably and relaxed.

CHECK-UP

Evaluate your writing for these elements of legibility:

Letter formation
Slant
Alignment and proportion
Line quality

Paper Position for Cursive Writing

LEFT-HANDED   RIGHT-HANDED

Rhythm in Writing

Write a definition for rhythm in handwriting.

Use practice paper.

Practice the following exercises. Glide on your last two fingers.

O O O

uuu   *lllll*   *lllleeee*

oooo   *aaaa*   *sssss*

Write the letters and letter combinations. Remember to use a full arm
movement for proper rhythm.

aaaa	*aiai*	*agag*
oaoa	*otot*	*onon*
lilili	*lyly*	*lala*
owowow	*olol*	*ovov*
gogogo	*gigi*	*gngn*
mmm	*meme*	*momo*

Write each word three times on practice paper. Underline your best writing of each word.

minimum   *upper-case*

maximum   *lower-case*

Pencil Position

POINTS TOWARD LEFT ELBOW

LEFT-HANDED

PENCIL NEAR BIG KNUCKLE

HOLD THE PENCIL WITH FIRST TWO FINGERS AND THUMB FIRST FINGER ON TOP

BEND THUMB

LAST TWO FINGERS TOUCH PAPER

POINTS TOWARD RIGHT SHOULDER

RIGHT-HANDED

Joinings

UNDERCURVE TO UNDERCURVE	UNDERCURVE TO DOWNCURVE	UNDERCURVE TO OVERCURVE
le	*ha*	*lm*

Write each joining and word three times on practice paper.
Underline your best writing of each joining and word.

le	*ha*	*lm*	*life*	*had*	*palm*
it	*co*	*dy*	*hit*	*come*	*daddy*

OVERCURVE TO UNDERCURVE	OVERCURVE TO DOWNCURVE	OVERCURVE TO OVERCURVE
ji	*yo*	*gy*

Write each joining and word three times on practice paper.
Underline your best writing of each joining and word.

ji	*yo*	*gy*	*jib*	*you*	*gyro*
ge	*jo*	*gy*	*get*	*joke*	*crazy*

CHECKSTROKE TO UNDERCURVE	CHECKSTROKE TO DOWNCURVE	CHECKSTROKE TO OVERCURVE
bl	*oa*	*wn*

Write each joining and word three times on practice paper.
Underline your best writing of each joining and word.

bl	*oa*	*wn*	*blue*	*oats*	*own*
we	*vo*	*on*	*well*	*vote*	*won*

48

A Dozen Doubled
by Dorothy Waldo Phillips

I'm thankful for my <u>shaggy</u> dog,
And for my <u>funny</u> speckled frog;
For crispy <u>carrots</u> that you munch;
For soda crackers that you crunch;
For baby robins in the spring;
For pop-up toasters going BING;
For every rainbow, snake, and snail;
For milk by <u>glass</u> or by pail.

I'm thankful for the sea and sand;
For teachers who can understand;
For <u>glowworms</u>, zoos, and jumping beans;
For <u>pussywillows</u>, kings, and queens;
For <u>happy</u> hoptoads by the lake;
For muffins and for bread I bake;
For autumn leaves all crispy red;
For all the time I'm out of bed.

Write the underlined words on practice paper.

Write the second verse of this poem on practice paper.

I'm thankful for the sea and sand;
For teachers who can understand;
For glowworms, zoos, and jumping beans;
For pussywillows, kings, and queens;
For happy hoptoads by the lake;
For muffins and for bread I bake;
For autumn leaves all crispy red;
For all the time I'm out of bed.

Joinings

The upper-case letters **A**, **C**, **E**, **H**, **J**, **K**, **M**, **N**, **R**, **U**, **Y**, and **Z** always connect to the letter that follows.
Write the words on practice paper.

Archery   *Kayak*

Cycling   *Marathon*

Equestrian   *Rowing*

Judo   *Yachting*

The upper-case letters **D**, **F**, **L**, **O**, **P**, **Q**, **V**, **W**, and **X** never connect to the letter that follows.
Write the words on practice paper.

Discus   *Pole Vault*

Lacrosse   *Water Polo*

The upper-case letters **B**, **G**, **I**, **S**, and **T** may or may not join.

Example:

Bowling   *Bowling*

Write the words on practice paper.

NOT JOINED	JOINED
Swimming	*Swimming*
Ice-skating	*Ice-skating*
Track	*Track*
Basketball	*Basketball*
Gymnastics	*Gymnastics*

50

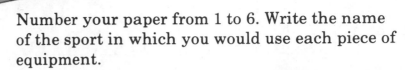

Number your paper from 1 to 6. Write the name of the sport in which you would use each piece of equipment.

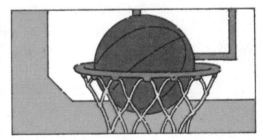

1

2

3

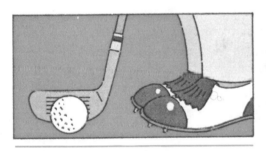

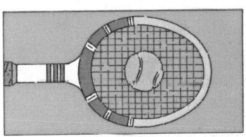

4

5

6

Write a paragraph about a sport you like. Include equipment and skills you would need and any safety measures you should take. Use practice paper.

For example:

For a game of basketball you need two teams of five players each. The object of the game is to throw the ball through a basket on the opponent's side of the court. The game requires much practice, skill, and teamwork.

Circle all the upper-case letters in your writing.
Are they formed correctly?

51

Manuscript Elements

Write the limerick in manuscript. Use practice paper.

A lively young fisher named Fischer
Fished for fish from the edge of a
fissure.
A fish with a grin
Pulled the fisherman in.
Now they're hunting the fissure for
Fischer.

Remember these rules for manuscript spacing:

The widest space is between straight-line letters.

Pulled

The least amount of space is between circle letters.

moon

Leave enough space between words to insert a lower-case **o**.

lively●young

Paper Position Manuscript Writing

LEFT-HANDED   **RIGHT-HANDED**

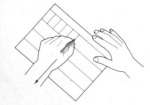
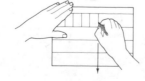

CHECK-UP

Evaluate your writing for these elements of legibility:

Letter formation
Vertical quality
Spacing
Alignment and proportion
Line quality

Work Wanted Ads

Look at the work wanted ads. Write an ad seeking work you might like to do. Remember times available, fees charged, equipment available, and locations suitable. Use manuscript writing. Write on practice paper.

Disc Jockey -Music from Bach to Rock! Available on weekends. Have own lighting and sound equipment. References available. Call (517)- 555-6774

Jr. Camp Counselor. Experienced. Dependable. Excellent references. Available July 1 in Wayne County Area. Tel.(513)- 555-7101

Here is a model:

Baby Sitter. Days or evenings during July and August. References. $1.75 per hour. Call 555-5707.

Cost of Placing an Ad

Classified Department
RATE SCHEDULE: Fifteen words for $1.25 plus 8 cents for each additional word per insertion. Count words, abbreviations, and numbers. No advertisement inserted for less than $1.25. Telephone 717-555-3055

Calculate the cost of placing each ad. Compute problems on practice paper.

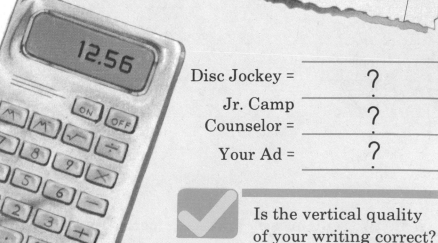

Disc Jockey =	?
Jr. Camp Counselor =	?
Your Ad =	?

Is the vertical quality of your writing correct?

53

Punctuation

. , ? ! ; : ' " "

Write the sentences on practice paper. Include the correct punctuation.

Teacher How would you punctuate this
sentence-- I saw a five-dollar bill on the
street
Student I'd make a dash after it

Bill Have you lived here all your life
Jill Not yet

Write the riddles on practice paper. Write answers for them.

I occur once in every minute, twice in
every moment; yet I never occur in a
thousand years. What am I?

What begins with t, ends with t,
and has t inside?

Write two sentences on practice paper, using as many different punctuation marks as you
can: period, comma, question mark, exclamation mark, semicolon, colon, apostrophe,
quotation marks.

Palindromes:

Palindromes read the same forward and backwards.

Write these palindromes with correct punctuation. Use practice paper.

pullupifipullup

madamimadam

risetovotesir

poordanisinadroop

wasitacatisaw

A palindrome can be a sentence or a word. Write as many words as you can that are palindromes. Some examples are shown below.

tot   noon   peep

mom   dad

Making Paper

Most paper is made from wood. The wood comes mainly from pine, spruce, hemlock, and fir trees. The logs are debarked and then chewed into chips by a machine. Next a digester tank cooks the chips into a brown stock. The brown stock is washed and screened until it is the color of brown paper bags. Now we have wood pulp.

Write the paragraph in your best writing. Use practice paper.

The following countries lead the world in the production of paper,

paperboard, and wood pulp. Write the names on practice paper.

United States	*Sweden*
Japan	*Finland*
Canada	*France*
U.S.S.R.	*China*
West Germany	*Italy*
United Kingdom	*Norway*

Paper products come from wood. What must the

manufacturers of these products do to make sure

there will always be paper in future years?

Evaluate your writing for these elements of legibility:

Line quality
Proportion
Letter formation

TREES

LOGS

CHIPS

DIGESTER TANK

If the paper is to be white, the pulp must be run through a bleacher. Now the pulp (either brown or bleached) is beaten until the fibers become sticky. Before the stock changes to a finished dry sheet, refiners get the exact stickiness needed. On a wire cloth diluted pulp is formed into a sheet. Water drains off, and the sheet is pressed, dried, and formed into giant rolls.

Which of the following are paper products? Write the words on practice paper.

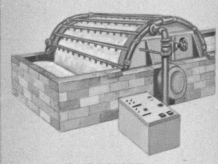

BLEACHER

mirror	dollar bills
books	greeting cards
compass	facial tissue
envelopes	cardboard box
newsprint	ballpoint pen
bags	stationery
magazines	thumbtack
calendar	gift wrapping
skillet	postage stamp

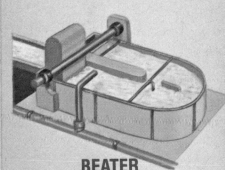

BEATER

Paper is everyone's servant. Write a paragraph to tell how

paper serves you.

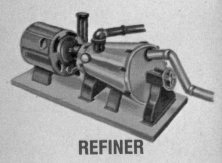

REFINER

 Evaluate your writing for these elements of legibility:

Slant
Alignment
Spacing

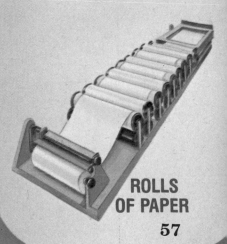

**ROLLS
OF PAPER**

Types of Literature

Write the words **Fiction** and **Non-Fiction** on practice paper. Read the definitions for each. Then choose three of the following titles to write under each heading.

The Boyhood of Thomas Jefferson
Treasure Island   American Democracy
Morgan Bay Mysteries   Famous Athletes
Encyclopedia Brown Finds the Clues

Fiction

Fiction is a literary work whose content is produced by the imagination and not necessarily based on fact.

Non-Fiction

Non-fiction is a literary work based on fact.

Paul Bunyan   Juliet   Fernando Valenzuela
Sandra Day O'Connor   Stevie Wonder
Robinson Crusoe   Mary Poppins   Golda Meir

Write the names of the characters under the correct heading. Use practice paper.

Fictional	Non-Fictional
Clues: a magical nanny	Clues: a baseball player
an over-sized lumberjack	a Supreme Court Justice
man on an island	singer and musician
Romeo's true love	a political leader

In which type of literature would you find the following sentences?
Write them on practice paper. Write **fiction** or **non-fiction** after each.

In 1922, the National Football League (NFL) was formed.

Now, what do you see? Why, the elephant shrunk to the size of a fat caterpillar!

Across the world, people are studying animal homing.

The Prince, dressed in leaves of gold, had sapphire eyes and a red ruby on his sword.

Fictional

Types of fiction: folk tales, myths, fantasy, realistic fiction, historical fiction, science fiction.

Write the titles of three fictional books you have read. Use practice paper.

Non-Fictional

Types of non-fiction: autobiographies, biographies, informational books.

Write the titles of three non-fictional books you have read. Use practice paper.

Review

Which of the following lower-case cursive letters begin with an undercurve? Write the letters on practice paper.

d   i   j   q   b   e   f   h   k   l   p   t   w   x

Which of the following upper-case cursive letters are always joined to other letters? Write them on practice paper.

C E A D H J L K Z M N O R U Y

Choose the letters that have the number of pauses indicated. Write them on practice paper.

no pauses   one pause

e   l   x   a   *b   c   d   a   l   f   g   h   i   j   n   t   y   g*

two pauses   three or four pauses

m   b   k   l   o   p   g   t   s   w   v   *y   w   r   f*

Write the following upper-case letters on practice paper. Circle the retraces.

A   B   F   G   H   M   N   P   R   S   W   Y

Write each letter. Write the numerical count for each. Use practice paper.

f   r   T   y
m   O   I   s
V   G   D   C
w   a   L   v

Write each letter joining on practice paper. Write the name of each joining.

it   ca   ga   oi   vy
an   ys   gg   bo   ft

60

Life of Liberty

Write the verse. Use practice paper.

"Give me your tired,
your poor,
Your huddled masses
yearning to breathe
free,
The wretched refuse of
your teeming shore.
Send these, the homeless,
tempest-tost to me.
I lift my lamp beside
the golden door!"

CHECK-UP

Evaluate your writing for
these elements of legibility:

Letter formation
Slant
Spacing

Alignment and
proportion
Line quality

Write the paragraph in cursive. Write on practice paper.

The oldest city in the United States is St. Augustine, Florida. Ponce de Leon, in search of the Fountain of Youth, landed in 1513 and took possession of the territory for Spain. The flags of Spain, France, England, the Confederacy, and the United States have flown over this territory.

✓ CHECK-UP

Evaluate your writing for these elements of legibility:

Letter formation
Spacing
Slant
Line quality
Alignment and proportion

Student Record of Handwriting Skills

Adult Proportion Cursive

PAGE		NEEDS IMPROVEMENT	MASTERY OF SKILL
4-5	Positions paper properly.	[?]	[?]
6-7	Demonstrates correct size and proportion.	[?]	[?]
8-9	Demonstrates correct spacing.	[?]	[?]
10-11	Demonstrates good line quality.	[?]	[?]
10-11	Demonstrates correct alignment.	[?]	[?]
10	Holds pencil properly.	[?]	[?]
12-13	Demonstrates correct slant.	[?]	[?]
16-17	Writes the letters **e, l, i, t, j** with the correct rhythmic motion.	[?]	[?]
18-19	Writes the letters **f, g, a, d, h, c** with the correct rhythmic motion.	[?]	[?]
22-23	Writes numerals.	[?]	[?]
24-25	Writes the letters **n, y, z, x** with the correct rhythmic motion.	[?]	[?]
26-27	Writes the letters **u, p, s, b, k** with the correct rhythmic motion.	[?]	[?]
28-29	Writes the letters **q, o, m, v, r, w** with the correct rhythmic motion.	[?]	[?]

PAGE		NEEDS IMPROVEMENT	MASTERY OF SKILL
32-33	Writes the letters **C, D, E, O** with the correct rhythmic motion.	[?]	[?]
34-35	Writes the letters **J, L, Q, V, Z** with the correct rhythmic motion.	[?]	[?]
38-39	Writes the letters **A, N, I, S** with the correct rhythmic motion.	[?]	[?]
40-41	Writes the letters **U, Y, K, X** with the correct rhythmic motion.	[?]	[?]
42-43	Writes the letters **H, M, P, R, G, T** with the correct rhythmic motion.	[?]	[?]
44-45	Writes the letters **B, F, W** with the correct rhythmic motion.	[?]	[?]
48	Writes undercurve, overcurve, and checkstroke joinings.	[?]	[?]
50-51	Writes upper-case joinings.	[?]	[?]
54	Writes legibly and uses properly the period, comma, question mark, exclamation mark, semicolon, colon, apostrophe, and quotation marks.	[?]	[?]

Book Six